Published by Stratford Living Publishing.
ISBN Print: 978-1-990332-60-9

Dedicated to my favourite Auntie

If you enjoy picnics as much as we do...

This story is a warning -about what NOT to do!

Picnics at a table can be a lot of fun!

But it's all about loca-tion loca-tion loca-tion!

So, we decided to have our picnic by the sea...

To celebrate the visit of my favourite Auntie.

proud
AUNT

We packed so much food, it was hard to close the trunk and then...

When we finally arrived at the beach we unpacked it all again!

"Let's picnic in the grass near the sand," Auntie suggested with a happy sound.

While Mommy and Auntie laid the food out, we played in the sand which was golden brown.

Soon enough it was time for us to eat!

We washed our hands (but not our feet!)

Then all we wanted to do was EAT EAT EAT!

Having a picnic lunch at the seaside was such a treat!

Auntie as our guest, chose her food first.

She decided on stinky liverwurst!

She prepared it carefully, putting it onto a bun.

Then she added mayo, pickles and some stinky cheese...

And finally her smelly bun was done!

An ant jumped onto the slice of cheese...It didn't seem to mind the smelly smell!

It scampered around like it was under a spell!

I wanted to yell

and jump to my feet!

To say,
"Auntie don't eat!"

But before we could warn her...

She took a bite!!!!

We watched her chewing the ant which wasn't a pretty sight!

Finally I jump jump jumped and said, 'Auntie you ate an ant!"

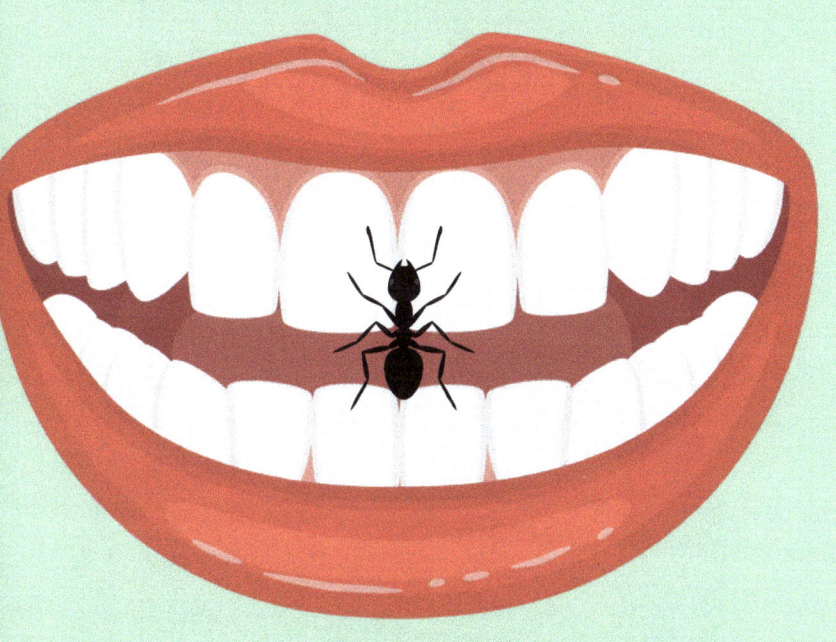

Instead of crying she licked her lips and said, "I've eaten chocolate ants before..."

"Don't worry!
It won't hurt me to eat
one more!"

It was then I started itching and scratching! It was like my skin was hatching!

I ran and JUMP JUMPED JUMPED INTO THE WATER! WOULDN'T YOU?

If you had...
Ants in your pants, OH NO!
Ants in your pants, OH NO!
What would you do?

Nex t thing I knew my family was with me in the water too!

And as the ants marched on we all started singing what we knew to be true...

"We've got ants in our pants,
OH NO!
Ants in our
pants,
OH NO!"

When we finally returned to our picnic...

Our picnic
by the sea...

Our table cloth and food were covered in ants.

An Anthill!!
No wonder we all had
ANTS IN OUR PANTS!

So, we put the blanket and basket into the trunk.

After shaking out the sand and ants and junk!

The moral of this story as we drove away...

Be sure to check for ants and anthills on Picnic Day!

At home there was just one thing left for us to do...

JUMP, JUMP, JUMP

BECAUSE OUR AUNT
ATE AN ANT!

We don't

AUNTS EATING ANTS

or

ANTS IN OUR

PANTS!

Other books in the
Jump Series:
Jump Like a Caribou!
Jump Like a Kangaroo!
Jump at the Zoo!
Jump and Say P.U.!
Jump and Say Boo!
Jump and Say Valentine's Day Is
For Kids Too!
Jump and Look For a Clue
Jump and Say Happy Birthday to
You!
Jump For Everything Blue!
Jump and Say Cock-A-Doodle-Do!

Jump and Squawk Like a Cockatoo!
Jump and Ask Is It Ewe?
Jump and Say There's an Ewww in My Stew!
Jump and Cheer Happy New Year!
Jump, Hop and Say Happy Easter To You!
Jump and Say There's A Moo-Moo in A Tutu!
Jump and Say There's A Hare in My Hair!

The Three Boulders
Billy Shakespeare
Billie Shakespeare

NON-FICTION
103 Fundraising Ideas For Parent Volunteers With Schools and Teams